Christian Crafts from Hand-Shaped Art

by Mary McMillan

illustrated by Veronica Terrill

Cover by Vanessa Filkins

Shining Star Publications, Copyright © 1991
A Division of Frank Schaffer Publications, Inc.

ISBN No. 0-86653-629-9

Standard Subject Code TA ac

Printing No. 151413121110

Shining Star Publications
23740 Hawthorne Blvd.
Torrance, CA 90505

Unless otherwise indicated, the New International Version of the Bible was used in preparing the activities in this book.

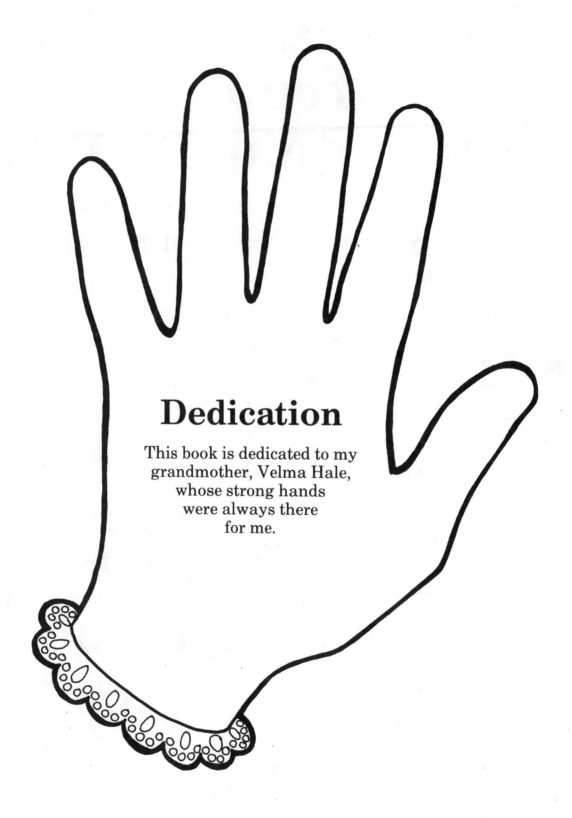

Dedication

This book is dedicated to my
grandmother, Velma Hale,
whose strong hands
were always there
for me.

Table of Contents

To the Teacher/Parent

Each project in this book requires a simple handprint. Yet, each single handprint is a unique distinctive creation of our Lord.

As the children complete projects, the projects themselves become personal reflections of the children of God.

Guide the children. Praise their work. And share the Bible scriptures related to each piece of art. But above all, allow the Bible teachings to come alive through the children's simple little handprints.

Materials required for the art projects in this book include construction paper, crayons, markers, pens, pencils, paints, glue, scissors, glitter, hole punch, cotton balls, clothes hangers, tissue paper, pipe cleaners, tagboard, sticks, balloons, yarn, and string. Some handprints have been provided for your convenience.

Have fun as you lift up your hands in His name!

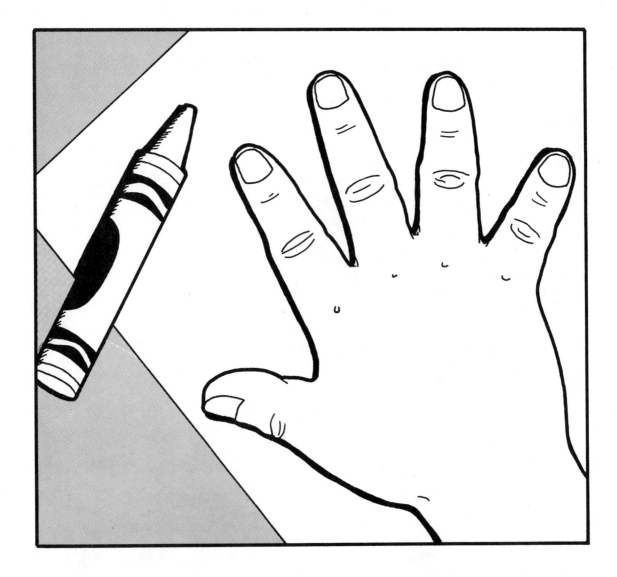

Noah's Ark

"male and female, came to Noah and entered the ark, as God had commanded Noah."   Genesis 7:9

Materials:

    Brown and blue construction paper
    Black crayons, marker, or pen
    Glue
    Water-diluted paint
      (suggested colors:
              monkeys-brown
              elephants-gray
              giraffes-orange
              Noah-pink or brown)

Directions:

1. Trace two handprints on brown construction paper. Draw horizontal lines with dark crayons, marker, or pen across each handprint to represent wooden planks in the ark.
2. Cut out. Glue the palm ends, labeled A in diagram, to a piece of blue construction paper.
3. Glue the fingertip edges together to form a three-dimensional effect on paper.
4. Have each child dip his fingertips into a water-diluted paint solution and place as many as seven fingerprints on each ark made. (Carefully clean and dry the children's fingertips before continuing.)
5. Instruct the children to draw faces on the fingerprints to represent Noah and the animals.
6. Add waves in the ocean with dark pen, crayon, or marker.
7. Display the artwork in outer hallways for all to see.

A   A

Angel of God

"Last night an angel of the God whose I am and whom I serve stood beside me"

Acts 27:23

Materials:

    White construction paper
    Thick white drawing paper
    Silver or gold glitter
    Glue
    Scissors
    Markers
    Hole punch
    String
    Pattern

Directions:

1. Trace two handprints on white construction paper.
2. Cut out and glue one to the other along the thumb sections.
3. Dilute the glue with water. Paint the handprints with the glue solution. Shake silver or gold glitter over the handprints to make angel wings.
4. Trace the angel figure and reproduce on thick white drawing paper. Use bright markers to color.
5. Glue the angel figure to the center of the overlapping thumb sections.
6. Hang the angels from ceilings, doorways, windows, or Christmas trees as holiday decorations.

SS1886

Rainbow

"I have set my rainbow in the clouds, and it will be the sign of the covenant between me and the earth."   Genesis 9:13

Materials:

Light-weight tagboard
Red, orange, yellow, green, blue, purple paint
Paintbrushes
Scissors
Glue and/or tape
Cotton balls
Clothes hangers
String
Pattern

Directions:

1. Trace the rainbow pattern (see page 9) and two handprints on a piece of light-weight tagboard.
2. Paint the rainbow with rainbow colors. Let dry.
3. Cut out the patterns.
4. Glue one handprint to each end of the rainbow. Glue cotton balls on the handprints to represent clouds.
5. Glue or tape the rainbow and clouds to a clothes hanger. Glue a cotton ball on the tip of the clothes hanger to cover the sharp point.
6. Use string to hang the hanger from the ceiling to share God's covenant of the rainbow.

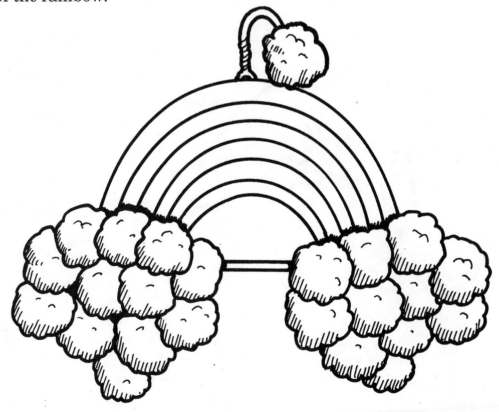

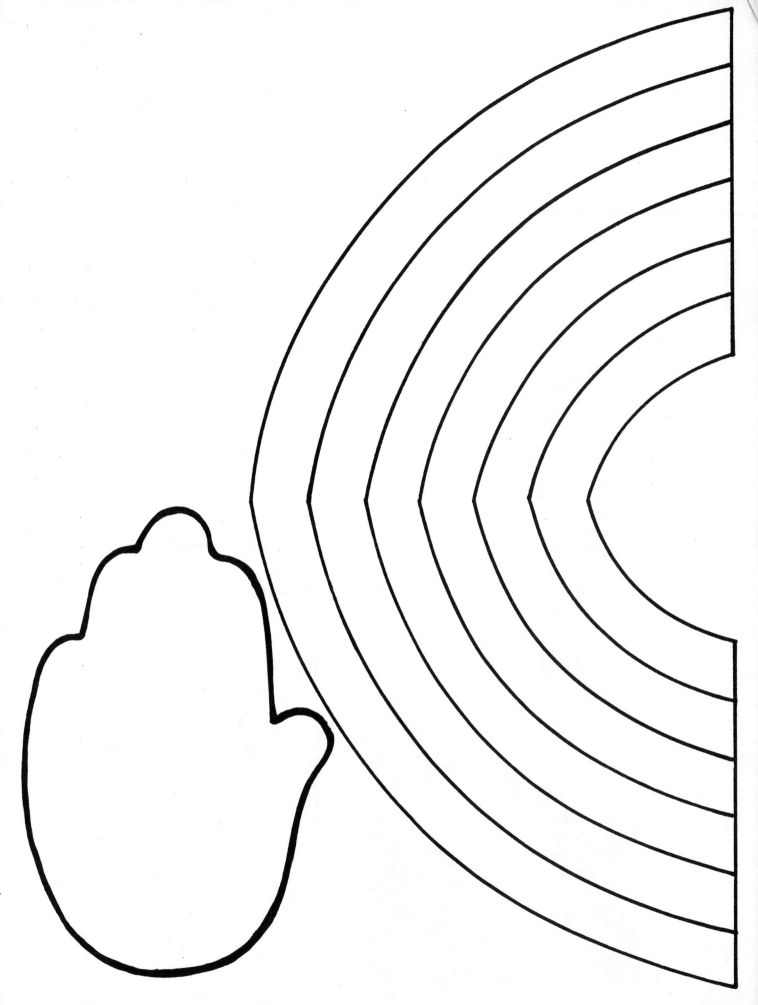

Candle Flame

"Your throne, O God, will last for ever and ever; . . ."   Psalm 45:6

Materials:

    Black and white construction paper
    Red, orange, and yellow tissue paper
    Brown yarn
    Scissors
    Glue
    Pattern

Directions:

1. Provide each child with a sheet of black construction paper.
2. Provide each with a candle pattern drawn on white construction paper. Cut out. Glue to the bottom half of the black construction paper.
3. Draw one handprint on each of the colored tissue papers. Cut out. Glue one over the other to form the flame above the candle.
4. Glue brown yarn between the tissue flame and the paper candle to represent the wick.
5. Display artwork to share God's word.

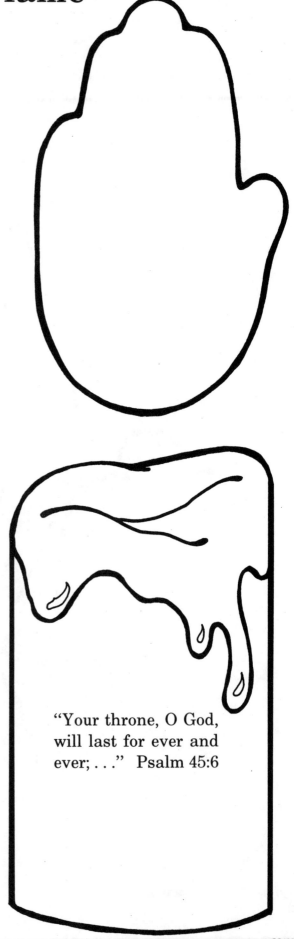

"Your throne, O God, will last for ever and ever; . . ." Psalm 45:6

Caterpillar

"And your spoil shall be gathered like the gathering of the caterpillar: . . ."
Isaiah 33:4 (KJV)

Materials:

Light-green and red construction paper
Dark-green paint
Red marker
Brown pipe cleaners
Glue
Pattern

Directions:

1. Paint the children's hands green. Have the children make five hand-prints across a piece of light-green construction paper, one overlapping the other, to form the caterpillar's body.
2. Provide the children with a caterpillar face pattern, reproduced on red construction paper. Cut out and glue to front end of the caterpillar.

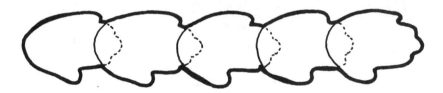

3. Use a red marker to draw dots along the caterpillar body.
4. Supply the children with two brown pipe cleaners apiece. Cut the pipe cleaners into seven pieces and glue one piece at the end of each thumb section, and glue two pieces to the head section to represent antennae.

   SS1886

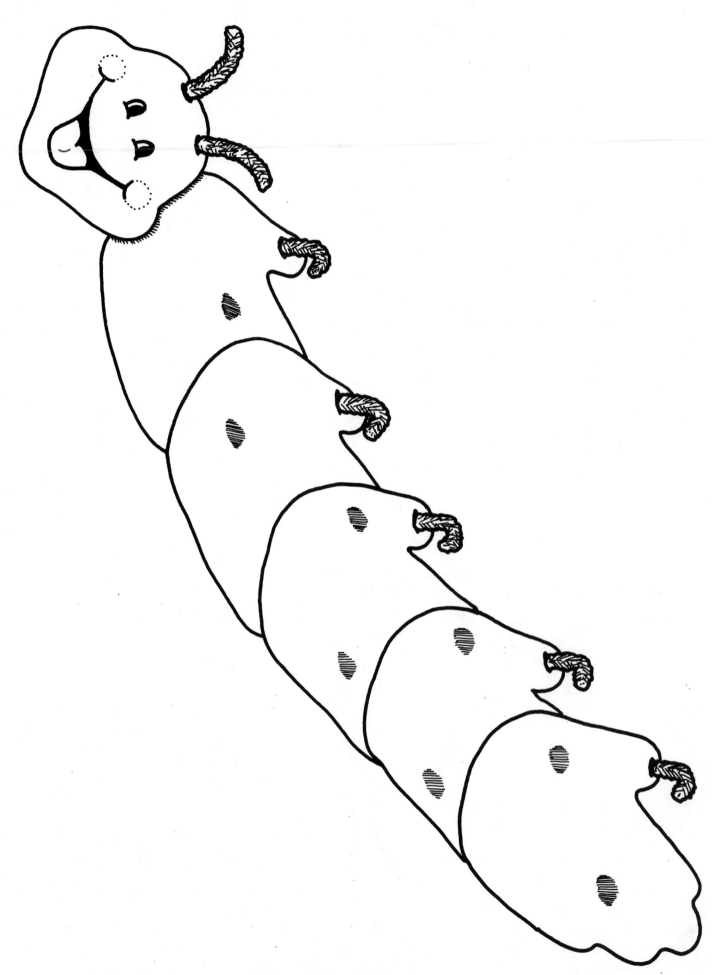

12

SS1886

Beasts

"God made the wild animals according to their kinds, the livestock according to their kinds, and all the creatures that move along the ground according to their kinds. And God saw that it was good."

Genesis 1:25

Materials:

    Tagboard
    Patterns
    Crayons or water-based markers
    Scissors
    Glue
    Rulers or sticks
    Cotton balls

Directions:

1. Trace the handprints on tagboard. Color and cut out.
2. Color and cut out the animal parts. Glue to the handprints to form animals.
3. Tape or glue to a ruler or stick to make a hand puppet.

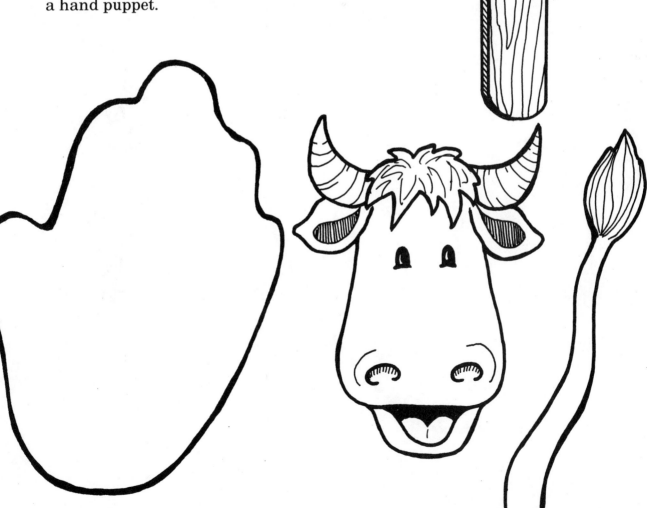

SS1886

"... 'Look, the Lamb of God, who takes away the sin of the world!' "
John 1:29

(Glue cotton balls over the animal to resemble lamb's wool.)

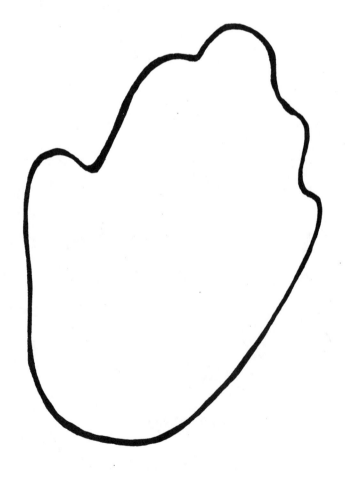

"My God sent his angel, and he shut the mouths of the lions. They have not hurt me, . . ."   Daniel 6:22

SS1886

"Again I tell you, it is easier for a camel to go through the eye of a needle than for a rich man to enter the kingdom of God."   Matthew 19:24

(Camel's body takes two handprints.)

Church

"...Christ is the head of the church, ..."   Ephesians 5:23

Materials:

    Patterns
    Brown and black construction paper
    Yellow crayon or marker
    Assorted crayons or markers
    Glue
    White paper

Directions:

1. Reproduce patterns A and B (see page 19) on white paper for each child.
2. Cut out pattern B and glue it to a piece of black construction paper.
3. Color the cross with yellow crayon or marker.
4. Trace two handprints on brown construction paper. Cut out and glue in the center of the white pattern B.
5. Cut out pattern A. Color it with a yellow crayon or marker. Glue over the bottom half of the handprints.
6. Reproduce ten face circles for each child. Color, cut out, and glue to each fingertip in the church scene.
7. Place the artwork near the entrance to the sanctuary to help spread the word of God.

"... Christ is the head of the church, ..."

Ephesians 5:23

A

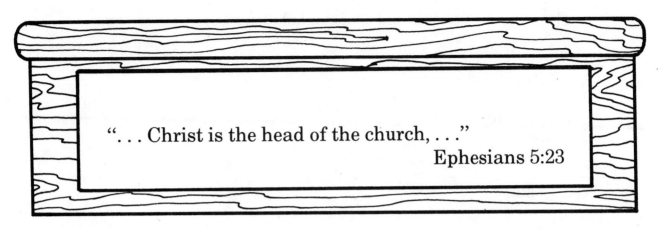

"... Christ is the head of the church, ..."

Ephesians 5:23

B

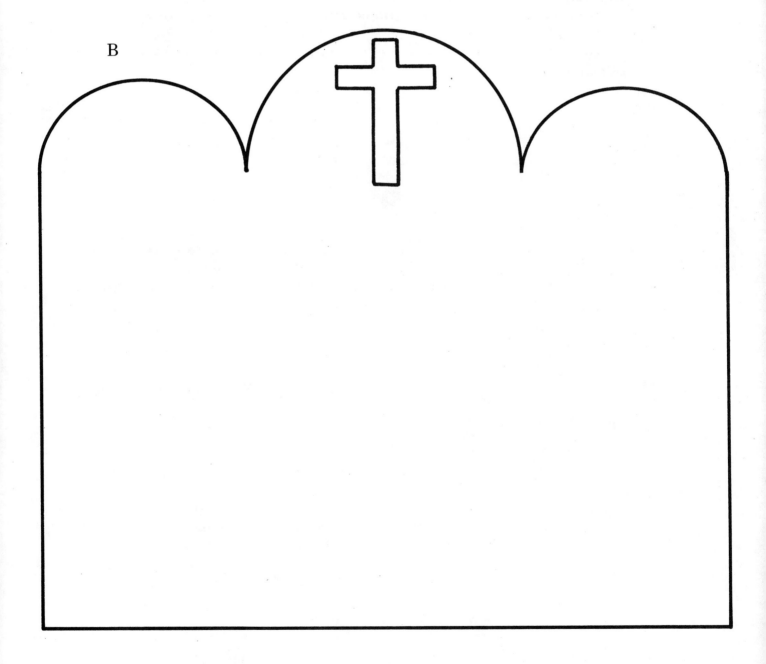

Butterfly

The butterfly is often used as a symbol of our Lord's resurrection.

Materials:

    Brightly colored construction paper
    Black paint
    Colored paints
    Popsicle sticks
    Glue
    Tape
    Safety pins

Directions:

1. Trace four handprints on brightly colored construction paper.
2. Cut out and glue the thumb sections together to form butterfly wings (see page 21).
3. Paint the Popsicle sticks black. Let dry. Glue to the center of the paper butterfly wings.

4. Paint circles, squares, and triangles on the wings to decorate. Let dry.
5. Tape or glue safety pins to the back sides of the Popsicle sticks.
6. Give to your mother, grandmother, or a friend to be worn as a pin to symbolize the resurrection of our Lord.

21

Shepherd

"The Lord is my shepherd, I shall not be in want."   Psalm 23:1

Materials:

    White drawing paper
    Black construction paper
    Crayons or water-based markers
    Scissors
    Glue
    Patterns
    Background scene

Directions:

1. Reproduce one background scene (see page 23) on white paper for each child. Have the children color their scenes.
2. Reproduce one set of shepherd and sheep patterns on white paper for each child.
3. Have the children trace around four fingertips and one thumb on the black construction paper. Cut out.
4. Color the shepherd. Cut out and glue to the thumbprint.
5. Color the sheep. Cut out and glue to the fingerprints.
6. Arrange the shepherd and sheep on the background scene and glue.
7. Display the pictures to spread the word of God.

"The Lord is my shepherd,
I shall not be in want."
Psalm 23:1

"The Lord is my shepherd,
I shall not be in want."
Psalm 23:1

Praying Hands

"I will praise you as long as I live, and in your name I will lift up my hands."

Psalm 63:4

Materials:

Light-weight tagboard
Crayons
Scissors
Glue
Heart-shaped helium balloons

Directions:

1. Trace two handprints on light-weight tagboard.
2. Color and cut out.
3. Glue one handprint over the other to form praying hands.
4. Write the Bible scripture and "See You in Church" message on the outside of each handprint.
5. Attach praying hands to the heart-shaped helium balloons with string.
6. Let the balloons go to spread the word of God all over your city.

glue

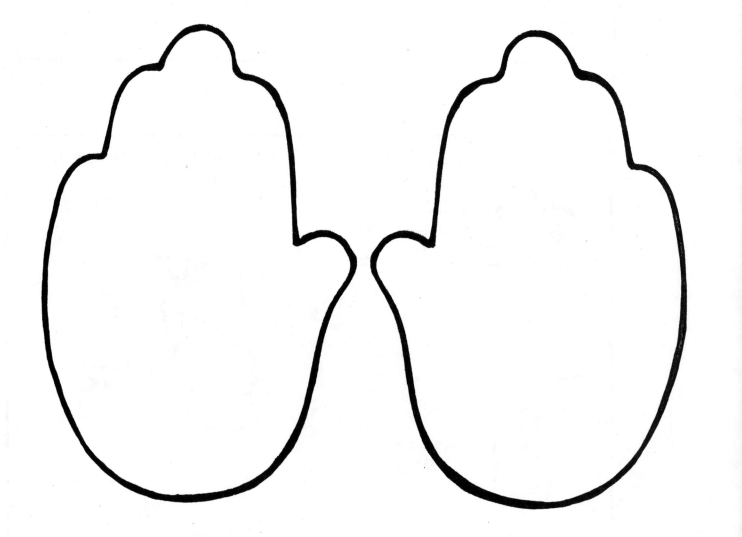

"... in your name I will lift up my hands."
Psalm 63:4

See you in Church on Sunday!

SS1886

Love Necklace

"...Love each other as I have loved you."   John 15:12

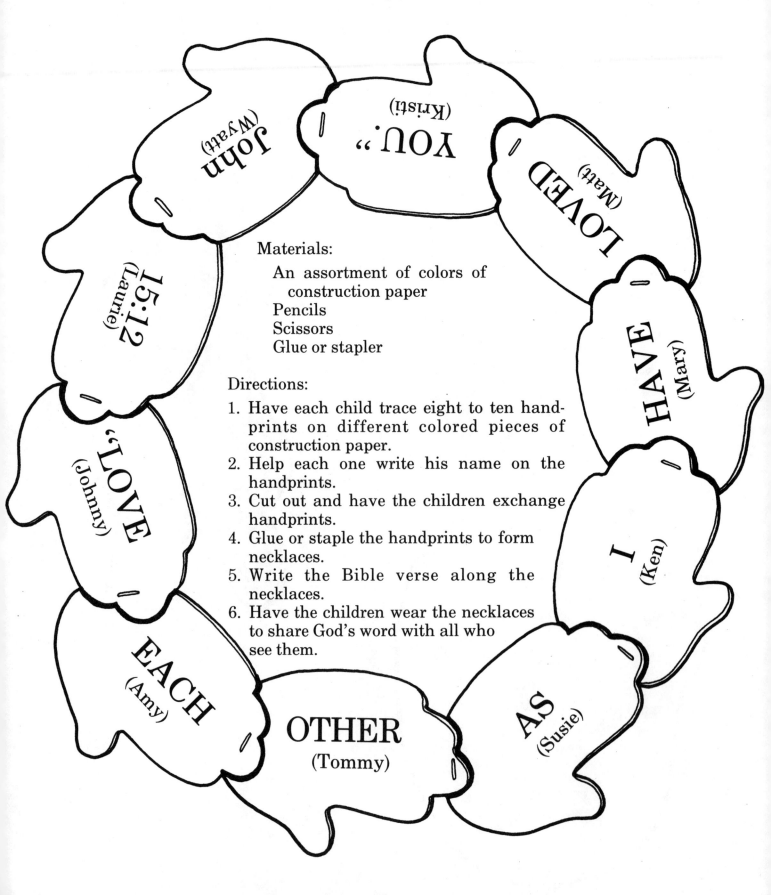

Materials:

An assortment of colors of
  construction paper
Pencils
Scissors
Glue or stapler

Directions:

1. Have each child trace eight to ten hand-prints on different colored pieces of construction paper.
2. Help each one write his name on the handprints.
3. Cut out and have the children exchange handprints.
4. Glue or staple the handprints to form necklaces.
5. Write the Bible verse along the necklaces.
6. Have the children wear the necklaces to share God's word with all who see them.

Cross

". . . take up his cross and follow me."

Matthew 16:24

Materials:

    Two 8″ paper plates
    Pattern
    Crayons or paints
    Pencils
    Scissors
    Glue
    Hole punch
    Ribbon

Directions:

1. Reproduce one cross pattern (see below) for each child.
2. Color or paint the cross. Cut out and glue to the center inside of one paper plate.
3. Color or paint the bottom side of the other paper plate. Let dry.
4. Trace one handprint in the center of the painted paper plate.
5. Cut out the inside of the handprint.
6. Apply glue to the inside front rim of the painted paper plate and fasten it to the other paper plate with the cross showing through the handprint.
7. Punch two holes at the center top of the plates. Run colored ribbon through the holes and tie.
8. Hang on wall to display God's holy word.

". . . take up his cross and follow me."

Matthew 16:24

SS1886

"...take up his cross and follow me."
Matthew 16:24

Bird's Nest

"Like a bird that strays from its nest is a man who strays from his home."
Proverbs 27:8

Materials:

    White and brown construction paper
    Scissors
    Glue
    String
    Hole punch
    Pattern

Directions:

1. Reproduce one dove pattern for each child on white construction paper. Cut out.
2. Trace four to five handprints on brown construction paper. Cut out. Overlap one over the other and glue to form the nest shape.
3. Glue the nest over the bottom part of the white dove.
4. Punch a hole in the bill of the dove. Hang with string to display for all to see.

"Like a bird that strays from its nest
is a man who strays from his home."
Proverbs 27:8

SS1886

"Like a bird that strays from its nest is a man who strays from his home."   Proverbs 27:8

SS1886

Fish

" 'Come, follow me,' Jesus said, 'and I will make you fishers of men.' "
Matthew 4:19

Materials:

    Orange, white and blue construction paper
    Bubble patterns
    Shell patterns
    Scissors
    Glue
    Squares of panty hose
    Patterns

Directions:

1. Trace one handprint on orange construction paper. Cut out. Draw on an eye and fin with a black crayon or marker.
2. Glue the fish to the center bottom half of blue construction paper.
3. Reproduce bubble patterns (see page 32) for each child on white construction paper.
4. Cut out bubbles and glue to blue construction paper above the fish as shown in diagram.
5. Provide each child with a piece of panty hose material the same size as the blue construction paper. Apply glue around the edges and cover the fish scene by pressing around the edges of paper.
6. Supply each child with enough shell patterns to cover the entire edge of blue construction paper. Cut out and glue around the edge.

shell pattern

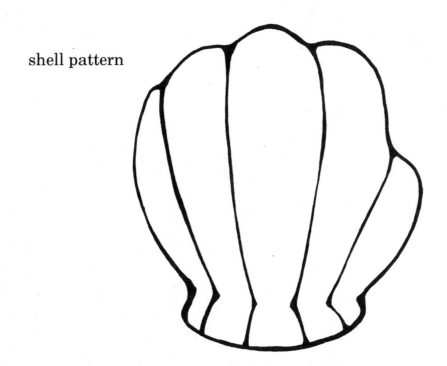

SS1886

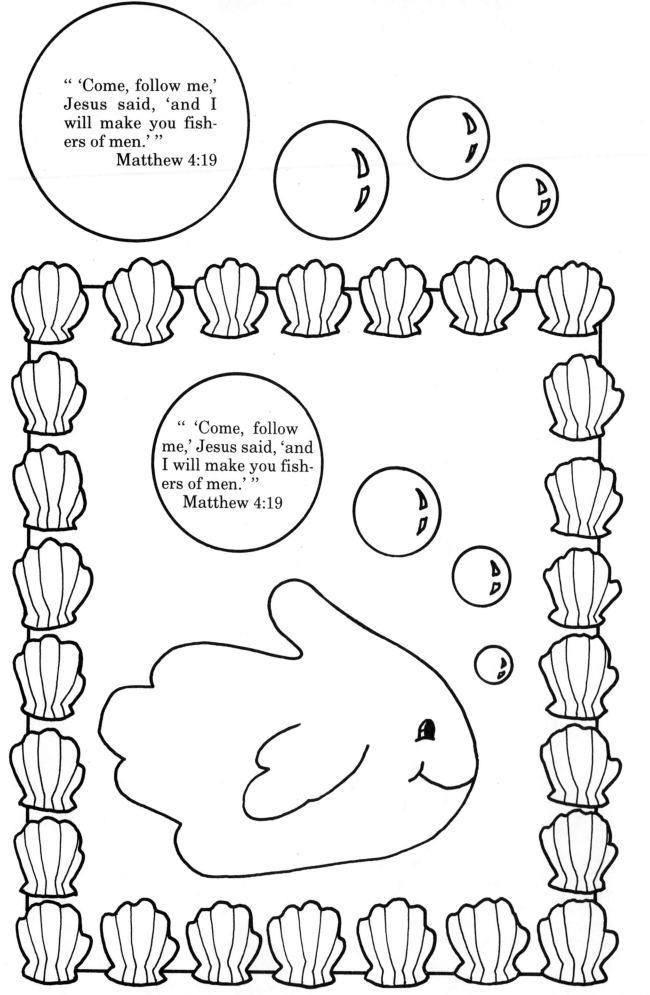

SS1886

Flower

" '. . . the grass withers and the flowers fall, but the word of the Lord stands forever.' "   I Peter 1:24, 25

Materials:

    Green, pink, red, yellow, purple, and blue construction paper
    Poster board
    Pencils
    Glue
    Scissors
    Yellow or brown pipe cleaners
    Pattern

Directions:

1. Reproduce two stem patterns (see page 34) on green construction paper for each child. Cut out. Glue one stem to each side of a piece of poster board cut the same size and length of each stem.
2. Trace two handprints on bright pink, red, yellow, purple, or blue construction paper. Cut out.
3. Take three 2″ yellow or brown pipe cleaner pieces. Glue one end of each pipe cleaner to one side of a handprint. Curl or bend the top part of each pipe cleaner to represent the flower stamens.
4. Glue the second handprint to the first handprint. Arrange the pipe cleaners and the top half of the stem between the two.
5. Have the children present the flower as a gift to help spread the Word of God.

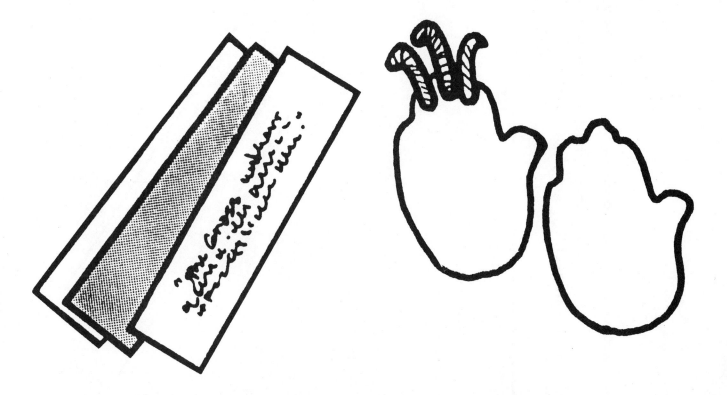

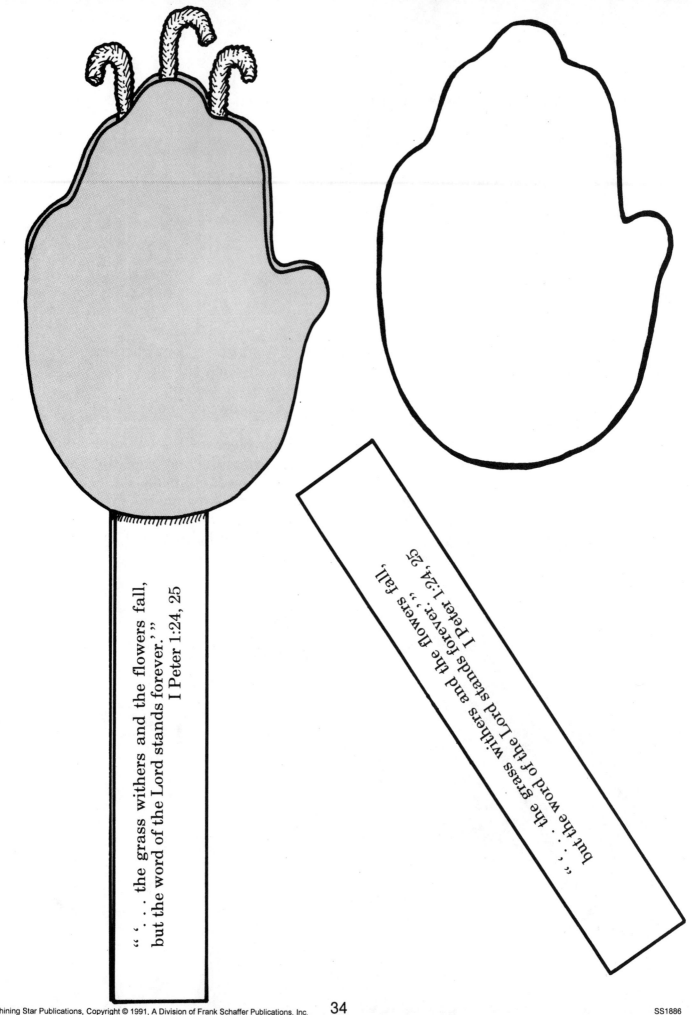

" '. . . the grass withers and the flowers fall,
but the word of the Lord stands forever.' "
I Peter 1:24, 25

" '. . . the grass withers and the flowers fall,
but the word of the Lord stands forever.' "
I Peter 1:24, 25

SS1886

Jonah and the Big Fish

"... and Jonah was inside the fish three days and three nights."

Jonah 1:17

Materials:

Jonah and the Big Fish color sheet
Crayons or markers
Blue construction paper
Pencils
Scissors
Glue

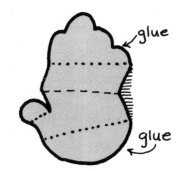

Directions:

1. Reproduce one Jonah and the Big Fish color page (see page 36) for each child.
2. Color with crayons or markers.
3. Trace five or more handprints on blue construction paper. Cut out. Fold up on .... lines. Fold down on - - - - lines.
4. Glue //// sections down to form waves in front of the whale. (see diagram.)
5. Display for all to see God's holy word.

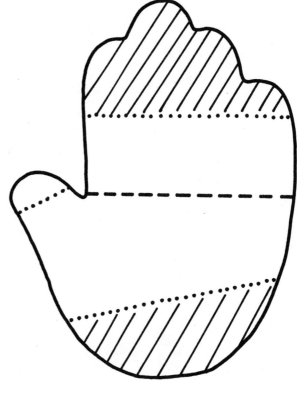

Jonah and
the Big
Fish

". . . and Jonah was inside the fish
three days and three nights."
Jonah 1:17

SS1886

Dove

"... and he saw the Spirit of God descending like a dove...."

Matthew 3:16

Materials:

Pattern
White construction paper
Pencils
Scissors
Glue

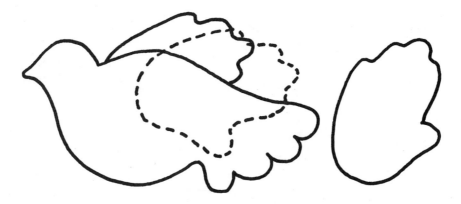

Directions:

1. Reproduce one dove pattern (see page 38) on white construction paper for each child and cut out.
2. Trace two handprints on white construction paper and cut out.
3. Glue the handprints on each side of the dove to represent wings.
4. Display as a symbol of the presence of the Holy Spirit.

SS1886

38 SS1886

Scripture Card

"Be still, and know that I am God; . . ."   Psalm 46:10

Materials:

   Red, pink, black, and brown construction paper
   White typing paper
   Scissors
   Glue
   Fine tip black marker
   Pattern

Directions:

1. Trace the mouth pattern on red construction paper. Cut out and glue to the center of the top half of typing paper.
2. Trace a handprint with fingers and thumb closed with only the index finger extended. Cut out and glue in the center of the typing paper with the index finger over the mouth pattern.
3. Fold the sides of the typing paper as shown in diagram on the following page to form a card.
4. Use a fine tip black marker to write the Scripture on the front of the card and ShShSh on the inside of the card.
5. Present the Scripture card to a friend to help spread the word of God.

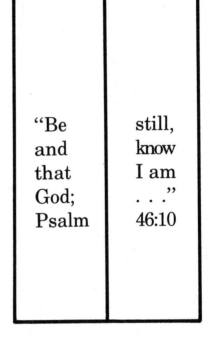

"Be and that God; Psalm   still, know I am . . ." 46:10

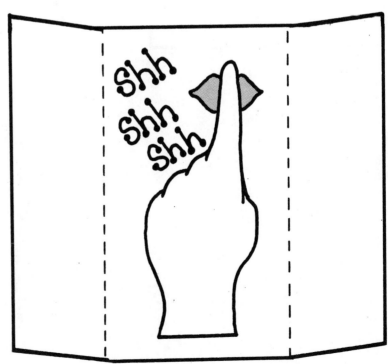

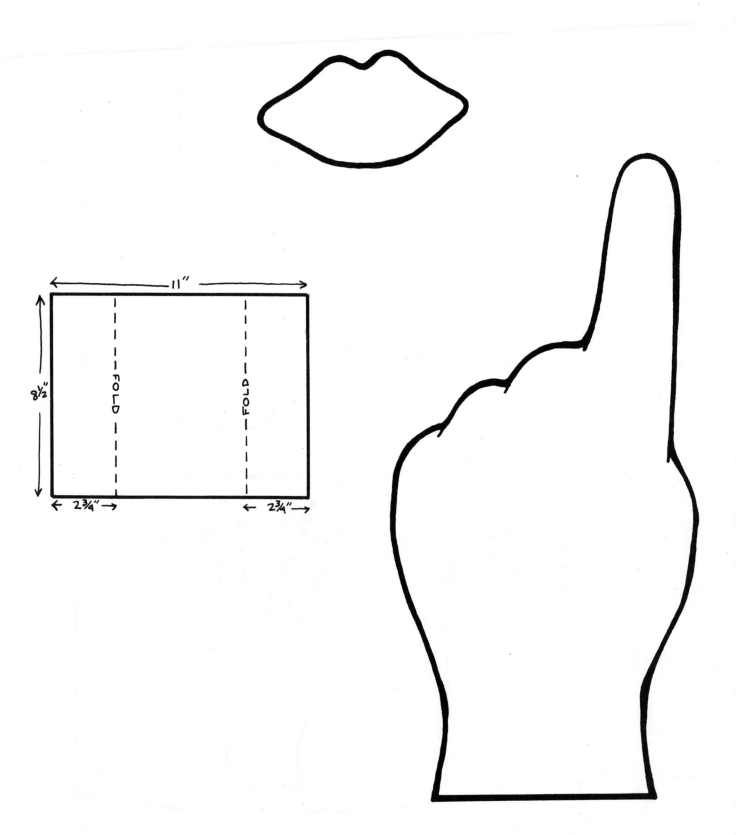

11"

8½"

FOLD

FOLD

2¾"

2¾"

SS1886

Joseph's Coat of Many Colors

"...and he made him a coat of many colours."   Genesis 37:3 (KJV)

Materials:
   Light-weight tagboard
   White construction paper
   Crayons or markers
   Scissors
   Glue
   Patterns

Directions:
1. Provide each child with the pattern of Joseph (see page 42) drawn on a piece of light-weight tagboard. Cut out.
2. Trace a handprint with the fingers extended on white construction paper.
3. Color each finger with a different color.
4. Cut out the handprint and glue it over the boy pattern of Joseph. Cut out the collar pattern and glue it in place.
5. Use the Joseph doll to act out the story of Joseph after reading from the Bible.

collar

42

SS1886

The Boy Jesus in the Temple

" '. . . Didn't you know I had to be in my Father's house?' "

Luke 2:49

Materials:

Brown and white construction paper
White drawing paper
Crayons or markers
Scissors
Glue
Patterns

Directions:

1. Provide each child with patterns of Jesus and the temple priests (see page 44) drawn on white paper. Color each with crayons or markers and cut out.
2. Provide each child with the temple pattern reproduced on white construction paper. Cut out.
3. Trace a handprint on brown construction paper. Cut out. Glue to the center of temple pattern.
4. Glue one temple priest pattern on each fingertip.
5. Glue the Jesus pattern into place on each fingertip.
6. Write the Bible Scripture verse on the top of the temple and display for all to see.

Embroidered Cards

"Then little children were brought to Jesus for him to place his hands on them and pray for them. . . ." Matthew 19:13

Materials:

    Medium-weight cardboard or poster board
    Needle
    Yarn or colored thread
    Scissors
    Fine tip black marker

Directions:

1. Trace a handprint on medium-weight cardboard or poster board.
2. Thread a needle with colored yarn or colored thread and tie a knot in the end.
3. The teacher should place black dots along the outline of the handprint. Have the children push the needle in and out of the black dots to form the outline of the handprint.
4. Use a fine tip black marker to write the Bible Scripture at the bottom of the card.
5. Give as a gift to a senior citizen to share God's love.

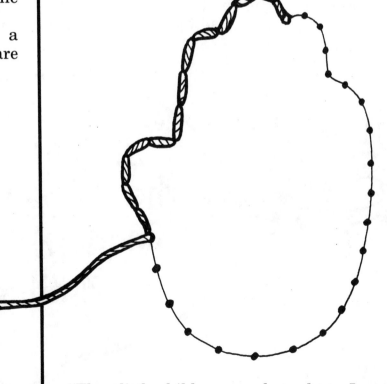

"Then little children were brought to Jesus for him to place his hands on them and pray for them. . . ." Matthew 19:13

Key Chain

"I will give you the keys of the kingdom of heaven; . . ."

Matthew 16:19

Materials:

Construction paper
Gray or gold water-based paint
Scissors
Glue
Hole punch
String or ball key chain
Black marker

Directions:

1. Trace six to eight handprints with fingers closed on a sheet of construction paper.
2. Cut out handprints.
3. Punch a hole at the end of the palm area on each print. Make sure the holes line up one over the other.
4. Glue the handprints one on top of the other. Let dry.
5. Paint the handprints with gray or gold paint to resemble a key. Let dry.
6. Use a black marker to write the Bible Scripture on the key.
7. Run a string or ball key chain through the holes.
8. Give to Mom or Dad for a key chain displaying the word of God.

Raindrops

"Again he prayed, and the heavens gave rain, and the earth produced its crops."

James 5:18

Materials:

    Large piece of blue paper
    White and green paper
    Yellow, white, green, blue paint
    Glue
    Black marker

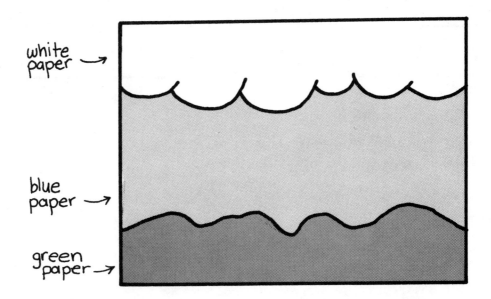

Directions:

1. Cover a wall area with a large piece of blue paper.
2. Cover bottom one-third of the blue paper with green paper.
3. Glue clouds cut from white paper to the top portion.
4. Paint the children's hands with blue paint. Press just below clouds to make handprints representing raindrops. The fingers should be together. Wash the blue paint from the children's hands.
5. Paint the children's index fingers with green paint. Press firmly on green paper to make stems and leaves. Wash the green paint from the children's fingers.
6. Paint the children's fingers with white paint. Press firmly above the stems to form petals of flowers. Wash the white paint from the children's fingers.
7. Place small amounts of yellow paint in the centers of the white petals to complete the flowers.
8. Use a black marker to write the message of God in the clouds.

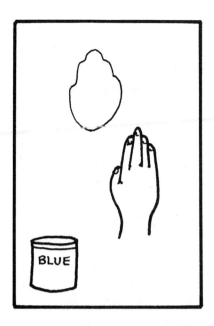

"Again he prayed, and the heavens gave rain, and the earth produced its crops." James 5:18

Grapes

"But the fruit of the Spirit is love, joy, peace, patience, kindness, goodness, faithfulness, gentleness and self-control. Against such things there is no law."

Galatians 5:22, 23

Materials:

Green and purple construction paper
Scissors
Glue
Black marker
Coin
Pattern

Directions:

1. Trace a handprint on purple construction paper and cut out.
2. Use the leaf pattern shown to trace a leaf and stem on the green construction paper. Cut out. Glue to the top of the purple handprint.
3. Trace around a coin to make nine grapes. Cut out. Glue over the purple handprint to form the grape cluster.
4. Use a black marker to write the Scripture on the grape cluster as shown in diagram.

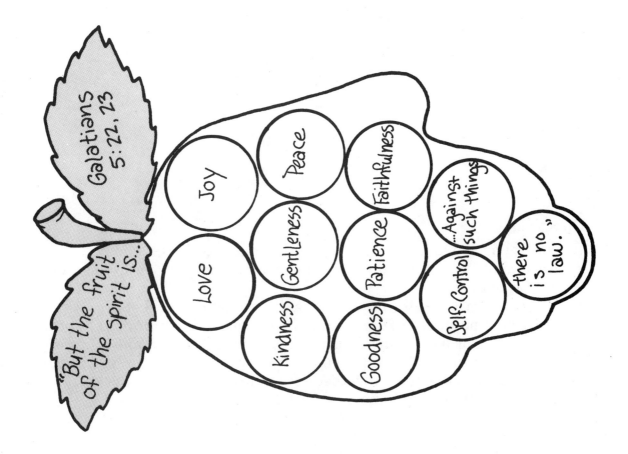

Friendship Belt

"I appeal to you, brothers, in the name of our Lord Jesus Christ, that all of you agree with one another . . ."   I Corinthians 1:10

Materials:
Tagboard
Scraps of fabric
Scissors
Glue
Hot-glue gun
Paint pen
Cloth paint pen

Directions:
1. Trace eight to ten handprints on tagboard and cut out.
2. Trace eight to ten handprints on an assortment of scraps of fabric and cut out.
3. Glue one fabric handprint to each tagboard handprint. Let dry.
4. Use a cloth paint pen to write one child's name on each cloth handprint.
5. The teacher or parent should use a hot-glue gun to glue one handprint to the other to form a belt. Leave an opening. Place the belt around the child's waist. Fasten together with a large colored paper clip.
6. Praise God by joining hands!

Shining Star Publications, Copyright © 1991, A Division of Frank Schaffer Publications, Inc.   SS1886

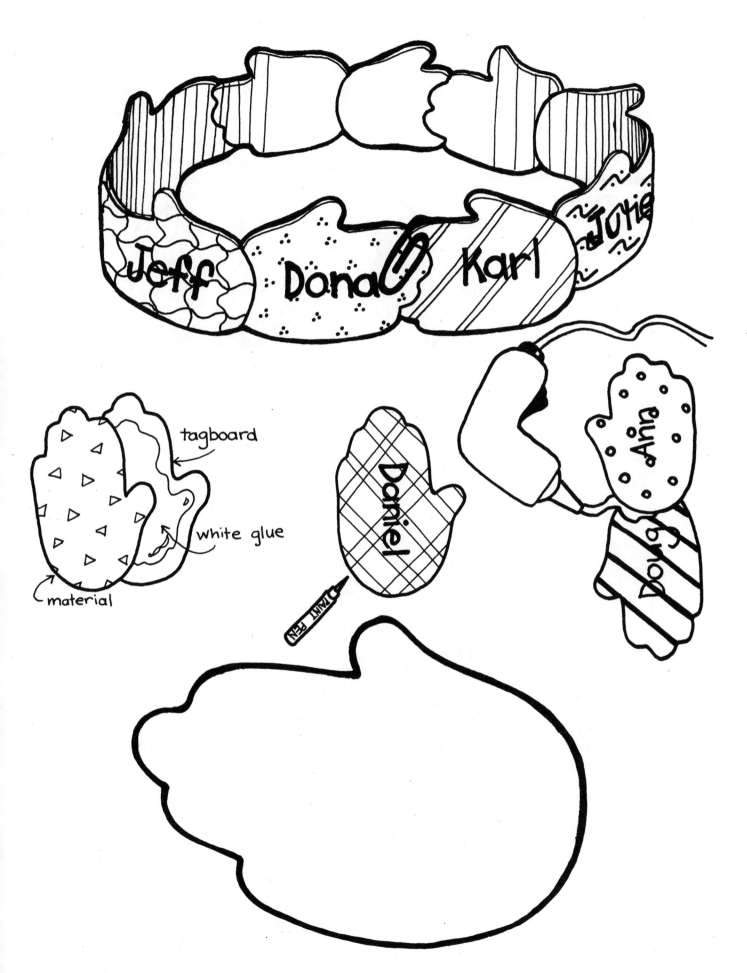

tagboard

white glue

material

Daniel

Tree

"The righteous will flourish like a palm tree, they will grow like a cedar of Lebanon;"   Psalm 92:12

Materials:

    Large piece of brown paper
    Bright green paper
    Scissors
    Glue
    Black marker
    Tape
    Stapler (optional)
    Pattern

Directions:

1. Reproduce a large tree trunk pattern as shown (see page 53). Cut out. Tape to an empty wall section in your classroom.
2. Have each child trace three to five handprints on the bright green paper and cut out. Tape or staple them above the tree trunk to form a flourishing tree.
3. Use a black marker to write the Bible Scripture on the tree trunk.
4. Read and discuss the Scripture with the children. Explain what it means to grow in God!

Shining Star Publications, Copyright © 1991, A Division of Frank Schaffer Publications, Inc.   SS1886

SS1886

The Sun

"God made two great lights—the greater light to govern the day and the lesser light to govern the night . . . ."   Genesis 1:16

Materials:

    Large piece of blue construction paper
    Green, orange, yellow construction paper
    Scissors
    Glue
    Black marker
    Patterns

Directions:
1. Trace four handprints on yellow construction paper and cut out.
2. Provide each child with the sun pattern (see page 55) drawn on yellow construction paper. Cut out.
3. Glue the sun pattern to the handprints to form the sun and its rays.
4. Give each child a large piece of blue construction paper.
5. Glue the sun to the top left-hand corner of the blue construction paper.
6. Provide each child with four to five flower patterns drawn on orange construction paper. Cut out. Glue them to the blue construction paper to make a flower scene.
7. Provide each child with the leaves and grass patterns (see page 55) drawn on green construction paper. Cut out. Glue to the blue construction paper to complete the flower scene.
8. Use a black marker to write the Bible Scripture.
9. Display artwork to share God's message.

55

Carrots

"...A man reaps what he sows."   Galatians 6:7

Materials:

    Large sheet of white paper
    Orange paint
    Brown, green, blue construction paper
    Scissors
    Glue
    Black marker
    Patterns

Directions:

1. Give each child a large sheet of white paper.
2. Paint the children's hands with orange paint. Press three to four orange handprints in a row near the bottom half of the white paper. Keep fingers closed tightly.
3. Trace three to four leafy patterns (see page 57) on green paper. Cut out. Glue to the tops of the orange prints to form carrots.
4. Trace a soil pattern (see page 57) on brown paper. Cut out. Glue over the finger sections of orange prints.
5. Trace the water pail (see page 57) on blue paper. Cut out. Glue above the carrot tops as shown in diagram.
6. Use a black marker to write the Bible Scripture. Display to share God's word.

The Twelve Apostles

"These are the names of the twelve apostles: . . ."   Matthew 10:2

Materials:

Tagboard
Crayons
Scissors
Glue
Wide red ribbon
Hot-glue gun (optional)
Patterns

Directions:

1. Enlarge and reproduce the Bible pattern (see page 59) on tagboard. Use a black marker to write the Bible verse. Then shade the pattern with a black crayon. Cut out.
2. Trace 12 handprints on tagboard. Use an assortment of crayons to color each and cut out.
3. Provide the apostles' name tags (see page 59). Cut out. Glue one to the center of each handprint.
4. The teacher or parent should use a hot-glue gun to glue the Bible pattern at the top of a long piece of wide red ribbon.
5. Use a hot glue gun to glue one handprint after the other down the ribbon to form a streamer. Cut away the excess ribbon at bottom.
6. Hang the streamer on a classroom door to help the children learn the names of Jesus Christ's twelve apostles.

John

Philip

Bartholomew

Simon Peter	Thomas	Judas Iscariot
Andrew	Matthew	Simon
James son of Zebedee	James son of Alphaeus	Thaddaeus

59

Apples

"A word aptly spoken is like apples of gold in settings of silver."
Proverbs 25:11

Materials:

Green and red paper
Cotton balls
Scissors
Glue
Hole punch
String
Patterns

Directions:

1. Make a fist. Trace two fist patterns on bright red paper and cut out.
2. Glue the two red patterns around the edges. Before completely closing, stuff center with cotton balls to make it three-dimensional.
3. Trace two leaf patterns on green paper and cut out. Glue together at the top of the red apple. Let dry.
4. Punch a hole in the top. Run a string through and hang.

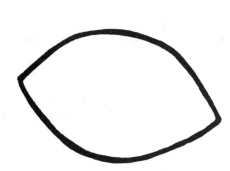

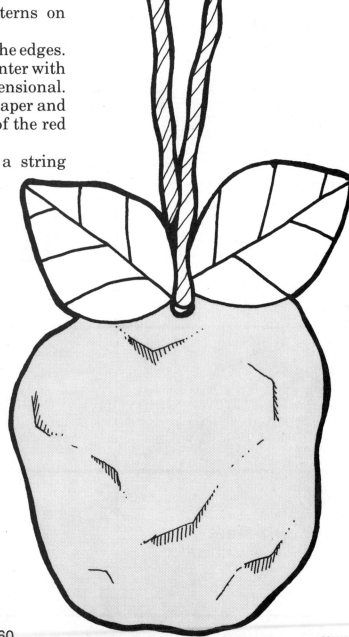

SS1886

Take Up His Cross

"... take up his cross and follow me."   Matthew 16:24

Materials:

    One 4-5″ diameter tagboard circle
    Two 4-5″ lengths of string
    Scissors
    Hole punch
    Markers
    Pattern

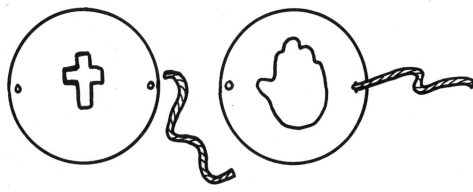

Directions:

1. Trace an open handprint on one side of a tagboard circle.
2. Trace and color in the cross pattern on the other side of the tagboard circle.
3. Punch a hole on each side of the circle. Run one piece of string through each hole and tie.
4. To 'take up cross,' twist the string between your thumbs and forefingers. Hold the strings taut to make the circle spin. The circle will turn rapidly, making the cross appear to be in the hand.

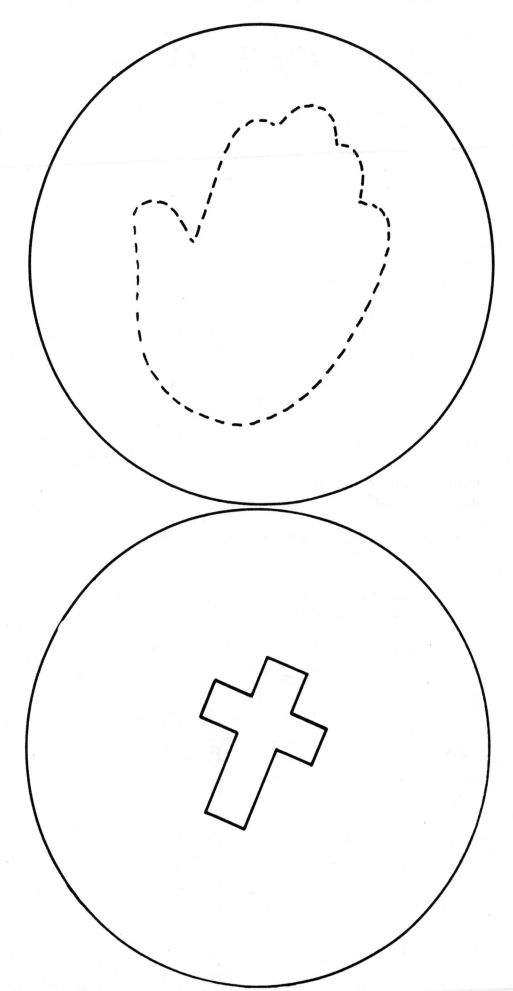

SS1886

Seashells Wall Mural

"...His rule will extend from sea to sea ..."   Zechariah 9:10

Materials:

   Large piece of white paper
   Brown and pink construction paper
   Crayons
   Scissors
   Glue or tape
   Black marker

Directions:

1. Tape or staple a large piece of white paper to a wall area.
2. Sketch the beach and ocean area as shown in diagram (see page 64).
3. Have the children color the beach area with light brown or beige crayons and the ocean with blue crayons.
4. Have each child trace one handprint on brown construction paper and one handprint on pink construction paper. Cut out. See diagram shown for folding the paper to form seashells.
5. Glue or tape the shells to the beach scene.
6. Use a black marker to write the Bible Scripture and share God's word.

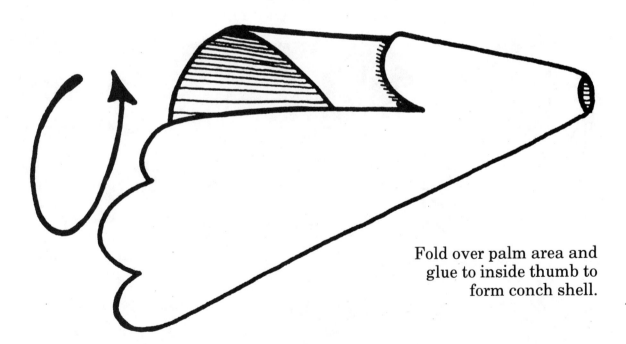

Fold over palm area and glue to inside thumb to form conch shell.

     SS1886

Seashells

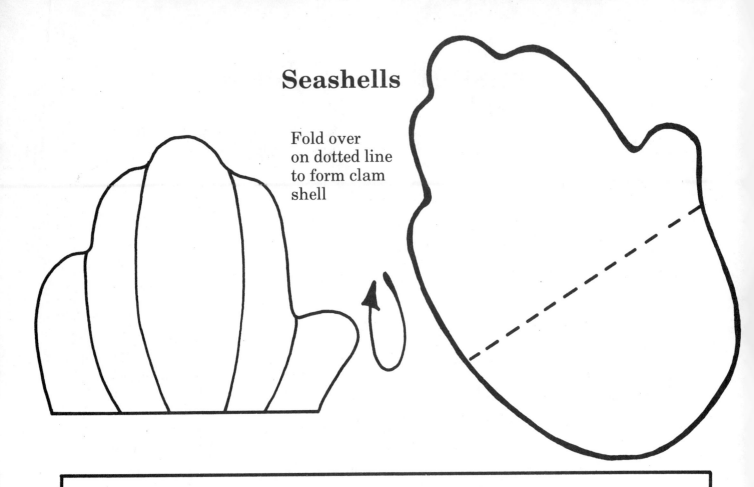

Fold over on dotted line to form clam shell

"... His rule will extend from sea to sea ..."
Zechariah 9:10